The Time Is At Hand!

The Time Is At Hand!

✦

An Introduction to the Book of Revelation

Desmond Ford

iUniverse, Inc.
New York   Bloomington

The Time is At Hand!
An Introduction to the Book of Revelation

iUniverse books may be ordered through booksellers or by contacting:

iUniverse
1663 Liberty Drive
Bloomington, IN 47403
www.iuniverse.com
1-800-Authors (1-800-288-4677)

Because of the dynamic nature of the Internet, any Web addresses or links contained in this book
may have changed since publication and may no longer be valid.

ISBN: 978-1-4502-0004-2 (sc)
ISBN: 978-1-4502-0008-0 (ebk)

Printed in the United States of America

iUniverse rev. date: 12/28/2009

Table of Contents

Introduction

○ ○

Blessed is the one who reads the words of this prophecy, and blessed are those who hear it and take to heart what is written in it, because the time is near.

Revelation 1:3[1]

This volume is the result of 70 years of thinking on the Bible's last book, including hours in the stacks of the Library of Congress handling its hundreds of commentaries on the book of Revelation. Add to that almost two years of intense study at the University of Manchester reviewing all eschatological parts of Scripture and the best commentaries about them. (Eschatology is the study of the final events in the history of the world and the ultimate destiny of humanity as taught in the Scriptures.) I have taught Revelation to College classes and other groups for over half a century. (This not a boast, but a confession of guilt because of the bypassing of many homely duties on the excuse of a passion to understand Scripture.)

My sad conclusion is that most that has been written on Revelation is worthless. Typical of the rubbish pile is Hal Lindsey's *The Late Great Planet Earth*, which has sold more than 20 million copies to gullible or uneducated readers, and which has never found acceptance with a single New Testament scholar esteemed by his peers. It may be that the reader of these pages will immediately consign my book to the pile mentioned above. I only request that he or she might read carefully and prayerfully.

The Apocalypse is not only the seal of Scripture but the mysterious Sphinx. Thomas Aquinas said, "If an ass looks into a book, you can't expect an angel to look out," and all of us are to a degree somewhat like the ass. The

---

[1] All Bible verses are NIV (New International Version) unless otherwise stated.

chief reason for failed exegesis of the last writing of the beloved Apostle John is that we all tend to look there for what is neither promised nor to be found there.

Almost all commentators have assumed that the purpose of Revelation is to set forth a preview or historical timeline of the more than 20 later centuries. Because of this, political and ecclesiastical events are sought out to fulfil the symbols of John. But nowhere does any part of the New Testament teach that the gap between the Cross of Calvary and the return of Christ had, of necessity, to be centuries long.

God always treats his people as though they will do the right thing, and from Matthew to Revelation the promise is repeated that our Saviour would return just as soon as the church took the gospel to the world. Furthermore, it is ever taught that this global proclamation could be accomplished in the first century of our era. See Matthew 10:23; 16:28; 24:34; Mark 13:30; Hebrews 9:26; 1:1,2; 1 John 2:18; 1 Corinthians 7:29,31; 10:11; Romans 13:12; 1 Thessalonians 4:15 and Revelation 1:1,3; 2:24,25; 3:3,10,11,20; 22:7,10,20 (these are all quoted at the end of the introduction). Observe that Paul expected many of the Thessalonians he addressed to be alive when Christ returned. Similarly consider the repetition of "you" in the Olivet sermon of Matthew 24, Mark 13, and Luke 21. The disciples were to see the things predicted.

A devout scholar of the nineteenth century summed up what most New Testament scholars would say today:

> Though time intervenes between Christ's first and second comings, it is not recognized … in the gospel scheme, but is, as it were, an accident. For so it was, that up to Christ's coming in the flesh, the course of things ran straight towards that end, nearing it at every step; but now, under the Gospel, that course has … altered its direction, as regards His second coming, and runs, not towards the end, but along it, and on the brink of it; and is at all times near that great event, which, did it run towards it, it would run into. Christ, then, is ever at our doors; as near eighteen hundred years ago as now, and not nearer now than then, and not nearer when he comes than now.
>
> Cited by Carl E. Amerding and W. Ward Gasque, eds., *Handbook of Biblical Prophecy*, p. 9

This quotation has great depth and is worth re-reading until we grasp the meaning. It means that what will happen has already happened (in theology this is called inaugurated and consummated eschatology). It distinguishes between the "now" and the "not yet," our status and our state. In the European view of history, there is a beginning and an end, and events require a punctiliar timeline. In salvation history, the final events have already happened in seed, and we live in that reality. The Bible sees the First Coming of Christ, his days on earth, his sacrifice, and the establishment of his Kingdom as occurring in the Last Days and the time of the end. Each generation of Christians since Calvary live in the time of the end, at the borders of eternity, and, so, the Second Coming is always imminent. There is a future Coming, but to understand Bible prophecy, one has to see the Second Coming as fused with the First and ever nigh.

As Jeremiah 18 clearly teaches, all God's promises and threatenings are conditional. So, Jonah could say quite bluntly that Nineveh would be overthrown in 40 days. But it was not overthrown. God could promise the generation taken out of Egypt that he would lead them into the Promised Land, but they died in the wilderness. Hezekiah was told he would die, but later he was given an extension of years.

It was a Semitic idiom to speak absolutely about matters that were understood to be contingent or conditional.

Revelation 17:10 is significant in this discussion. "They are also seven kings, five of whom have fallen, one is, the other has not yet come, and when he comes he must remain only a little while." The world power is on its last legs. But one more phase is to be manifested and it will exist only for a short time. Readers in the first century would have understood this verse exactly as it reads. The book of Revelation was written to nerve the church of that day to complete the gospel commission. Had the Jewish people repented (Acts 3:19-21), and the early Christians been faithful, they could have seen Christ return and been caught up together with him to heaven without passing through the portals of the tomb. Because this is so contrary to our traditional thinking, I suggest that the verses quoted above be read and reread.

Does all this render Revelation useless to believers of the twenty-first century? Not at all! This closing book of Scripture is an enlarged edition of the Olivet discourse. Remember John was the only one to write a Gospel lacking that sermon. All the elements of Christ's Second Advent sermon would be fulfilled over and over again in ever-larger concentric circles, until the final fulfilment just before his appearance in the clouds (see Ecclesiastes 3:15). Many prophecies are seminal with the capacity of repeated fulfilments. This process has been called the apotelesmatic principle.

Accompanying the error of believing that our book was intended to sketch the political and ecclesiastical events of over 20 centuries is the parallel presupposition that we have the right to look here for prominent figures of history and specific dates of important events. All this takes place, despite the very specific warning of Acts 1:7: "It is not for you to know the times or dates the Father has set by his own authority." Many claim to have found in the book of Revelation predictions of USA or the tiny survivors of Judaism. Some think Britain is here and its nineteenth-century opponent, Napoleon, or the later dictator, Adolf Hitler. More favoured perhaps than any other are the Pope or the monster of the first century—Nero.

But Revelation offers more important themes than any of these. The very first verse tells us that it is intended to be an unveiling of Christ, and before each major section of the book the Savior is portrayed symbolically. He is mentioned 137 times in the first three chapters, and the book bestows upon him 25 different titles. We are told that the very essence of prophecy, its burden, is testimony about Jesus and from Jesus. See Revelation 1:2 and 19:10. The central verses, Revelation 12:10-12, are about Christ, his kingdom, his gospel, and his church:

> Then I heard a loud voice in heaven say:
> "Now have come the salvation and the power and the kingdom of our God, and the authority of his Christ,
> For the accuser of our brothers who accuses them before our God day and night, has been hurled down.
> They overcame him by the blood of the Lamb and by the word of their testimony; they did not love their lives so much as to shrink from death.
> Therefore rejoice, you heavens and you who dwell in them!
> But woe to the earth and the sea, because the devil has gone down to you!
> He is filled with fury, because he knows that his time is short."
> Revelation 12:10-12

As we might expect, the Body of Christ, the Church, figures prominently in every chapter, and an important key to understanding this book is the recognition that the Body of Christ repeats the experience of its Head. The letters to the seven churches are a paradigm of the experiences of Christian churches in all ages.

In the Gospels, the great enemies of Christ are Satan, the degenerate church, and the State. In the heart of Revelation we find the same three. In chapter 12 Satan is named and is prominent, and in the following chapter we have the two beasts that respectively signify persecuting statecraft and degenerate religion allied to the State. In chapters 11, 12, and 13, is found the symbol of 1260 days or 42 months—reminiscent of Christ's ministry and several earlier crises. Even Antichrist, the first beast of Revelation 13, is:

> ... a travesty of the Lord Jesus Christ himself, the Head and King, and the Guardian and Protector, of his people. Like the latter, the former is the representative, the "sent" of an unseen power, by whom all authority is "given" him; he has his death and resurrection from the dead; he has his throngs of marvelling and enthusiastic worshippers; his authority over those who own his sway is limited by no national boundaries, but is conterminous with the whole world.

William Milligan, *The Book of Revelation*, p. 224

Most important of all is the fact that the primary purpose of Revelation is to warn the church of a coming worldwide Calvary immediately prior to Christ's return. See 6:11-17; 11:7-13; 12:17; 13:11-17; and 16:12-16. See the book *The Coming Worldwide Calvary* by the present author for more details.

Revelation is the last book of the New Testament. The Greek word for "testament" is used also and most often for "covenant." These last 27 books of the Bible belong to the new covenant. To understand the seven seals, the seven trumpets, and the seven last plagues, which occupy so much of the Apocalypse, we have to be familiar with the blessings and curses of the Mosaic covenant. See Deuteronomy chapters 28 and 29, and Leviticus 26. Knowing these chapters gives a key to these important forecasts.

Another presupposition on the part of many interpreters is to consider that this book is to be read literally. So Armageddon becomes the great plain of Palestine where so many major battles were fought, and Babylon becomes the name of a new city yet to be set up north of Palestine. But repeatedly we are given clues that the book is a book of symbols, all of which are to be unlocked. The keys are not modern events or existing geography, but the Old and New Testaments. At the very commencement we are told that the visions were "signified" (1:2, KJV). In other words they came in signs and symbols. See Revelation 11:8, which states precisely that figurative language is being employed. Otherwise we have to believe that Christ will come from heaven with a great sword projecting from his mouth as he rides a giant white stallion (see 19:11-16). Other incongruities include a woman sitting on a beast with seven heads (17:3) and a pregnant woman in heaven (12:2). Add to that last picture the sight of an angry dragon pursuing the woman through the heavenly courts, ultimately attempting to drown her by the emission from his mouth of a mighty river.

So in a few paragraphs we have endeavoured to question the vast majority of books claiming to interpret Revelation and to replace them with keys that are authentic and Christ-centred. Now let us leave controversy behind and major in what is positive and uplifting.

In the Apocalypse all the books of the Bible meet and end. Every promise, hope, prophecy and theme of the preceding 65 books here find their mature consummation. Without this book the Scriptures would be a house without a roof, or a story without a climax and conclusion. Revelation is the crown of Holy Scripture, as surely as are the records of our Lord's death in the Gospels. The interpretation of that event in Romans constitute its heart.

While the Gospels record Christ's coming in the flesh, and Acts his coming in the Spirit, this book tells of his return in glory. The Gospels speak of the Head of the church, and the Epistles of his Body, but this book speaks of the union of Head and Body. The Gospels have for their theme the Atonement, which brought our justification. The Epistles speak of this also, but spell out in greater detail the theme of sanctification, since God both justifies and sanctifies his saints. While justification and sanctification are distinct, they are never separate in the truly regenerate child of God. Without holiness, no man shall see the Lord.

The union of Head and Body in Revelation means glorification—corruption giving way to incorruption, mortality to immortality, and struggle and weariness to rest. Thus this concluding book of Scripture sets forth judgment, resurrection, and glorification, as well as the earth made new, with the banishment of sin and sinners forever.

> When you are persecuted in one place, flee to another. I tell you the truth, you will not finish going through the cities of Israel before the Son of Man comes.
> Matthew 10:23
>
> I tell you the truth, some who are standing here will not taste death before they see the Son of Man coming in his kingdom.
> Matthew 16:28
>
> I tell you the truth, this generation will certainly not pass away until all these things have happened.
> Matthew 24:34

I will tell you the truth, this generation will certainly not pass away until all these things have happened.
Mark 13:30

Then Christ would have had to suffer many times since the creation of the world. But now he has appeared once for all at the end of the ages to do away with sin by the sacrifice of himself.
Hebrews 9:26

In the past God spoke to our forefathers through the prophets at many times and in various ways, but in these last days he has spoken to us by his Son, whom he appointed heir of all things, and through whom he made the universe.
Hebrews 1:1,2

Dear children, this is the last hour; and as you have heard that the antichrist is coming, even now many antichrists have come. This is how we know it is the last hour.
1 John 2:18

What I mean, brothers, is that the time is short. From now on those who have wives should live as if they had none ... For this world in its present form is passing away.
1 Corinthians 7:29, 31

The night is nearly over; the day is almost here. So let us put aside the deeds of darkness and put on the armor of light.
Romans 13:12

According to the Lord's own word, we tell you that we who are still alive, who are left till the coming of the Lord, will certainly not precede those who have fallen asleep.
1 Thessalonians 4:15

The end of all things is near. Therefore be clear minded and self-controlled so that you can pray.
1 Peter 4:7

The revelation of Jesus Christ, which God gave him to show his servants what must soon take place. ...
Revelation 1:1

Blessed is the one who reads the words of this prophecy, and blessed are those who hear it and take to heart what is written in it, because the time is near.
Revelation 1:3

"Now I say to the rest of you in Thyatira. ... Only hold on to what you have until I come."
Revelation 2:24,25

"Remember, therefore, what you have received and heard; obey it, and repent. But if you do not wake up, I will come like a thief, and you will not know at what time I will come to you."
Revelation 3:3

"Since you have kept my command to endure patiently, I will also keep you from the hour of trial that is going to come upon the whole world to test those who live on the earth.

I am coming soon. Hold on to what you have, so that no one will take your crown."
Revelation 3:10,11

"Here I am! I stand at the door and knock. If anyone hears my voice and opens the door, I will come in and eat with him, and with me."
Revelation 3:20

"Behold, I am coming soon! Blessed is he who keeps the words of the prophecy in this book."
Revelation 22:7

Then he told me, "Do not seal up the words of the prophecy of this book, because the time is near."
Revelation 22:10

He who testifies to these things says, "Yes, I am coming soon."
Revelation 22:20

Chapter One

The Time Is at Hand!

○ ○

Blessed is he that readeth, and they that hear the words of this prophecy, and keep those things which are written therein; for the time is at hand.

Revelation 1:3, KJV

Read Revelation chapters 1-3.

All of us have experienced sin as a burden upon us, a tyrant over us, and a traitor within us. Justification deals with the first, sanctification the second, and glorification the third. In the Book of Revelation, it is promised that our old nature, which was legally crucified at the Cross and subdued in sanctification, is finally to be eradicated. Sinful propensities which afflict us here, causing us to cry out, "O wretched man that I am," will soon be no more. Hereafter there shall be no cruel gap between intention and achievement, between the ideal and the real (Revelation 22:2-4; 20:6; 21:4 and 14:5). No wonder Revelation is full of songs and doxologies. In the very first chapter we are reminded of the One who has loved us and loosed us from the captivity of sin by his sacrifice. Surely this joyous verse is a guide to what we should expect in all that follows.

Attempting to interpret this book is like trying to empty the sea with a teaspoon. To change the figure, Revelation is full of glorious manna, full and pressed down and overflowing in abundant measure. While Genesis is the seed plot, Revelation is the flowerbed. As Genesis spoke of creation, the marriage of the first Adam, the beginning of life, service, marriage, the Sabbath, sin, sorrow, death, Satan, Israel, and the covenant, so here in the Apocalypse we witness the new creation, the marriage of the second Adam,

1

the glorification of life and service, the true fellowship of souls and union with God—symbolized by marriage and the eternal Sabbath rest. As the third chapter of Scripture introduced evil, so the third last chapter bids it farewell. Revelation 20 forecasts the destruction of Satan, sin, sorrow, and death. God's Israel will enter upon all that the everlasting covenant promised of glory and joy. It is as though we have been travelling on a golden ring and returned to where we started. But it is the return of the octave at a higher, sweeter pitch.

The first section of Revelation has the same relationship to the rest of the book as Genesis does to the whole Bible. Everything to come is present in seed form in these first chapters. If we do our work well here, the way will be paved to understand all the rest. Sadly, the first chain, the letters to the seven churches, reveals a dimming of the gospel flame—an indication of the chief obstacle (sin) hindering the proclamation of the gospel.

What then are the themes of chapters 1-3? Christ, his nature and glory, his work, his salvation, his covenant, his kingdom, his coming, his people—these are the themes of this introductory section. Therefore, let us not look here, nor in the chapters which follow, for that which God has not promised. We shall find nothing here about calendrical dates, or secular powers (see Acts 1:7). There is no allusion to modern inventions or to anything belonging to our materialistic culture.

The opening chapter alludes to the Olivet Discourse, which was given to the miniature church, the disciples (for example, compare 1:7 with Matthew 24:30). That discourse was a commentary on Daniel 9:24-27—the great Old Testament prediction about Messiah the Prince—his coming, his being "cut off," his city, his people, his covenant, and his great antagonist, Antichrist. Daniel 9:24-27 itself is an explanation of the climactic verse of Daniel 8:1-14. Following that symbolism, all that is given to the seer of Babylon is interpretation (chapters 10 to 12).

This grand prophecy (Daniel 8 and 9) had foretold the undoing of sin, transgression, and iniquity, and the bringing in of everlasting righteousness, fulfilling all prophetic vision, in order that God might return to tabernacle once more with his people. This prophecy had promised all that the ancient Day of Atonement prefigured—judgment and abolition of sin and sinners, reconciliation between God and man with all sorrow past. The sanctuary, as a symbol of the kingdom of God, mirrored in its history the state of the covenant people. Christ, intimating his messianic task, cleansed the sanctuary at the beginning and end of his ministry. He himself was the new Temple, and because his people are one with him, they too throughout the New Testament are called the temple of God. With all this in mind, Revelation 1:12-20 and chapters 21 and 22 should be studied as the symbolic expression of the consummation of the sanctuary's covenant promises. The whole earth cleansed and renewed becomes the everlasting temple of God and the Lamb. Even the New Jerusalem is pictured as having the proportions of the Holy of Holies.

In Revelation, the same Christ who came to Daniel in captivity comes to John in exile in the new Babylonian empire—that of Rome. This first chapter describes him even as he appeared when he visited the writer of the Old Testament apocalypse. See Daniel 10. Now he comes as the Prophet, Priest, and King of that sanctuary spoken of in Daniel 8 and 9. He is the true Guardian of the temple courts, the Judge as well as the Saviour of all who walk therein. He trims the church lamps, and punishes with the sword of his mouth. He is preparing his people for glory, and those who will not be cleansed must be removed from their place. Judgment begins at the house of God, and this book of judgment upon the world begins with judgment upon the church. Chapters 2 and 3 find our Priest and kingly Judge examining the professions and walk of his people and proclaiming his verdict. All the promises made to the members of the seven churches are elaborations of the promises of Daniel 8:14 and 9:24. They have to do with the end of sin and the bringing in of everlasting righteousness.

Revelation chapters one to three remind us that trials and trouble are our lot here below. As the Church lets her light shine, opposition automatically results. Christ's witnesses are called to be faithful unto death; they like the Messiah are to be "cut off." Whenever the church is true to its commission martyrdom ensues, and the blood of the martyrs is the seed of the blossoming community until the whole earth is filled with God's glory. John, in this book—like Daniel in his—is the pattern for all believers. He has been faithful to the Word of God, the testimony of Jesus. At the grand old age of nearly a century we find the beloved apostle on the barren rocky isle that was one of the prisons of ancient Rome. But he is not alone—the Christ that he loves and serves arrives in glory to visit, strengthen, inform, and commission him.

Let us not ignore the challenge found in this record. Wherever the church sits at ease it has ceased to witness. Wherever the church fulfils her commission blood will flow. This entire book repeats that lesson repeatedly. A sinful world needs whistleblowers. Let us not ignore that as though true Christians could be comfortable in this world.

The visit of Christ takes place on the Sabbath—the Lord's Day. That day symbolizes the rest of Eden, the rest in Christ through dependence on his finished work. It is particularly appropriate that in this context the Sabbath should be mentioned. Over and over, we find reference to the Exodus in these verses, and the Sabbath was the sign of the Sinaitic as well as the Edenic covenant. The Old Testament, like the New, recognizes only one divine everlasting covenant, and the Prince who confirmed it on Calvary is the giver of the Patmos revelation.

These early verses teach that the New Testament church is the new Israel, and therefore any endeavour to read the experience of modern Jewry in this book is misplaced. Modern Jewry is still beloved for their father's sake, but they are Gentiles, strangers from the covenant of promise and need to be grafted in again to the tree of spiritual Israel, as all other Gentiles must. As a nation, the Jews have no special destiny. This was revoked when they cried, "We have no king but Caesar." Their Messiah previously had warned them, "The kingdom of God shall be taken from you and given to a people bringing forth the fruit thereof"—the Christian church.

The covenant allusions found in chapter one are repeated and multiplied throughout the rest of the book. We shall read of the Ark of the Covenant and its testimony—the Decalogue. The rainbow of the covenant will shine offering encouragement to those who must live through storm and tempest. The covenant curses of war, famine, pestilence, wild-beasts, and death are the key to the seals. The trumpets, the plagues, and the blessings of life, fruitfulness, joy, and rest will be traced in their fulfilment before we lay the book down. See Deuteronomy 28, 29 and Leviticus 26.

From the opening verses of this book, and repeatedly afterwards, we find legal words such as "testimony." All Christians echo the testimony of their Lord—the truths he testified before men and devils in Galilee, Jerusalem's streets, and the courts of Caiaphas, Pilate, and Herod. Christ witnessed a good confession, and it is the church's continual task to re-echo that. The proclamation of the gospel, the fulfilling of the Great Commission, is nothing other than telling the story of the Cross (1 Corinthians 2:2 and Galatians 6:14). This task fulfilled brings the Second Advent. Through the proclamation and pilgrimage of the Church God makes manifest to principalities and powers his manifold wisdom and power. See Ephesians 3:9,10. We are now a theatre to the universe, to angels, and to men. See 1 Corinthians 4:9 (original).

The church's message now is, "The hour of his judgment is come." The gospel itself rightly proclaimed is judgment. Compare Revelation 18:10. In the opening chapter of this book we find the word of God symbolized by a two-edged sword proceeding from the mouth of Christ. He promised that his word would judge all men at the last great day (John 12:48). Similarly, his Cross is the judgment of the world (John 12:31). On Calvary he separated the penitent from the impenitent. The word of the Cross does likewise. Men are judged by their response to the sacrificial love of God, and the last great day will declare it. Today is the day of salvation; today is the appointed time for acceptance. Today, if we hear his voice let us not harden our heart, for the hearing of the gospel itself brings judgment. Not so much the sin question, but the Son question, is the issue. What have we done with him?

Those at peace with God do not fear the coming of that Judge who has already absolved them with his gift of the ultimate verdict. Thus there is no need for panic theology such as is found in the work of Hal Lindsey. Believers see the Second Coming only through the lens of the First. When Christ is known as Saviour his relation as Judge brings no fear. Twenty-eight times in this book our Lord is set forth as the Lamb of God who has taken away the sin of the world.

It is a very profitable study to consider the seven major sections of Scripture that exalt the Lamb of God. In Genesis 3:21 the Lamb is typified; in 22:13,14 the Lamb prophesied; in Exodus 12:13 the Lamb's blood is applied; in Isaiah 53 the Lamb is personified; in John 1:29 the Lamb is identified; in Revelation 5:6-12 the Lamb is magnified; in Revelation 21 and 22 the Lamb is glorified. And inasmuch as the blood of the Lamb is so prominent in Revelation (1:5; 7:14; 12:11), we should also consider the first seven passages in the Bible where blood is specially emphasized. In Genesis 4:10 the blood cries; in 9:5,6 the blood is sacred; in 37:32,33 the blood is presented to the Father; in 42:22, there is a reckoning for the blood; in 49:11 we have the washing of garments by the blood; in Exodus 4:9, blood is the sign of the wrath of God; and in Exodus 12:13, blood is the only covering in the Judgment.

Before each prophetic chain the eye is made to rest upon Christ, our great High Priest. Only looking unto Jesus steadies us for considering what is to come upon the world. See Hebrews 12:2 and 3:1, Matthew 17:8 and Luke 4:20.

Revelation 1:7 is a key verse in the opening chapter of the book of the Second Coming, for it is this event which brings the end to sin, sorrow, pain, and death. The theme of 1:7 will meet us repeatedly throughout the book. To the churches Christ says: "If you will not watch, I will come on you as a thief"; "Behold, I come quickly." The seals climax in the great day of his coming and the question is asked, "Who shall be able to stand?" The trumpets picture the preliminary judgments upon the world, and close with the kingdoms of the world becoming the kingdom of Christ at his coming. In the final chapter of our book, our Lord assures us that he is "coming soon." Contrast the admonition given to John not to seal the book with that given to Daniel, which was the opposite. See Daniel 8:26 and Revelation 22:10. John is not to seal his book because the Coming is at hand.

If there is no final victory of good over evil, the kingdom of God becomes an empty dream (T.W. Manson). In the Christianity of preceding centuries, thanatology (the study of death) replaced eschatology. This error the New Testament never makes. It is not death that is "the blessed hope" of the believer. Over 300 times the New Testament speaks of the Second Coming, and that refrain now reaches a hallelujah chorus in Revelation. The New Testament generation believed they were in the Last Days and that Christ was about to appear. Had Judaism repented, and the infant Church done its work it would have been even so.

Following the prologue of the book, which repeatedly refers to Christ and his two advents we have the initial vision. This vision is the key to the whole book. As Ariadne supplied Theseus with a thread at the very entrance of the cavern he had to penetrate, so here John places a torch in the hand of the reader at the beginning of his search. The centre and circumference of this vision has to do with light.

We see Christ clothed with the sun, every part of him beaming with celestial glory, and he walks among the light holders—lampstands—and holds luminaries (stars) in his hand. The vision therefore speaks of the coming of light to displace the darkness—and this is the theme of the entire book. Christ is the light of the world. He shines through his church as it proclaims the gospel that alone can illumine the darkened soul. All that follows in this book will speak of the experience of the light-bearers, their progress, their opposition, and their ultimate triumph. The victory of the light will be imaged by symbols of conquest such as the white glistening horse. The sacrificial sword will portray the war of darkness against it. Light and darkness will alternate throughout the visions until we come to the city of light where there is no night, and where the Lamb is the eternal Sun.

All the warnings and promises of this book are conditional. The very timing of the Second Advent, viewed from one standpoint, is conditional. "Whosoever will may come." "Whoever is athirst may partake of the water of life freely." Christ stands at the door and knocks, but there is something for us to do. As Philippians 2:12,13 tells us, our salvation has been accomplished, but we must work it out. God does everything by way of holiness within our hearts, but we must work. Our destiny is assured if we continue to trust, but we are to fear and tremble lest we be seduced from him by our own carnality. There is no "once saved, always saved" in this book, nor anywhere else in Scripture.

Only acceptance and cherishing of the gospel will bring all things needed, including Christ's coming. Faith, penitence, righteousness, strength, missionary motivation and skill—all these are his gifts to those who see themselves as wretched, poor, blind, and naked, and therefore cry, "Even so, come Lord Jesus, come to this troubled heart today." And he does.

Chapter Two

Let Not Your Hearts Be Troubled

○ ○

After this I looked, and there before me was a door standing
open in heaven. And the voice I had first heard speaking to
me like a trumpet said, "Come up here, and I will show you
what must take place after this."

Revelation 4:1

Read Revelation chapters 4-7.

We have come to a new beginning. Chapters four and five are "the fulcrum of
the book," as well as the introduction to all that follows. They constitute one
of the key partings of the way for interpreters, for at this point the decision
must be made whether to accept the dispensationalist approach to the rest
of the book. This group considers that the secret rapture is indicated by the
words, "Come up hither." Futurists who reject dispensationalism, such as
G. E. Ladd, interpret the seals in principle in the same way as historicists.
Concerning the first four seals, Ladd says they picture the character of the age
and its relationship to the kingdom of God.

Significantly, the theme of these two chapters is God—the Father, the
Spirit, but especially the Son. As the seer was given a vision of heaven and
not physically transported there, we will need to keep in mind that it is not
heaven itself that he is reproducing, but the symbols of it shown to him. If
we get lost in the drapery and minutia of the vision, the true meaning will
escape us. Not the twenty-four elders, not the four living creatures, nor the
glassy sea, but the Redeemer is the focus. The chapters are a commentary on
the words of the departing Christ, "Let not your hearts be troubled, ye believe
in God, believe also in me."

Chapter four points particularly to God the Creator, and five to Christ the Saviour. Jesus is saying," Be of good cheer, the Father himself loves you, and because I live, you shall live also." How appropriate this theocentric setting is for the revelations that follow—revelations of the messianic woes set forth in terrifying imagery!

It is not tragedy that humans cannot endure; it is tragedy without meaning. These chapters shout the truth that there is nothing without meaning, that there is neither chance nor accident, for God is on the throne, and with him the One who suffered on Calvary for his rebel children. This is a far cry from the fears of Thomas Hardy about "The dreamy, dark, dumb Thing that turns the handle of this idle Show." We are here introduced to the magnificent drama of the sovereignty of God. But it is more. It is the drama of redemption.

As the previous section began with a reference to the throne of God (1:4) and closed by mention of the throne of Christ (3:21), the fourth chapter presents the throne of the Father, and then the fifth reveals that Christ also shares that throne. "Throne" is one of the key words of this book, occurring 40 times out of the 57 occurrences in the New Testament. Seventeen times it is found in these two chapters, which introduce the rest of the book. Not Domitian, the threatened church is assured, but God is supreme Sovereign.

> "Under the shadow of thy throne
> Thy saints have dwelt secure;
> Sufficient is thine arm alone,
> And our defense is sure."

Before the winds of strife are loosed, before the apocalyptic horsemen ride forth, before the trumpets are blown, before the great tribulation of the final Calvary is pictured, we see the throne, not only of our Creator, but also of Him who is also Redeemer. So the afflicted churches of John's day and their successor in our time find assurance that at the centre of the universe there is neither chaos nor steel, but a heart—not only divine but human and full of sympathy.

For this reason—the fact that love rules the universe—these chapters are filled not only with mystery, but also with song. Three great doxologies assure us that one of the main businesses of heaven is praise. When Isaiah contrasted his own stammering tongue with the adoring announcements of the angels, he knew himself to be unclean. That praise is as much a duty as prayer has not fully registered with any of us. How can one boast of perfection while praise commensurate with its Object remains a virtually unknown tongue?

Chapters one to three described the internal and external problems of the Church—that Church which was to make possible the return of Christ by its proclamation of the gospel to all the world. Some of the lamps were portrayed as giving only a clouded flame. What then lay ahead for this church, which though enfeebled and defective, was still the supreme object of God's regard? How would it endure the trauma of battle? What is to be its destiny? And what also is the destiny of the world, which presses it so cruelly? It is the purpose of this section to begin the answer to these questions.

The first thing John sees in this vision is a throne—but it is clearly a throne of judgment. From it flare flashes of lightning, and peals of thunder. The whole scene is reminiscent of Daniel 7:9-13 where "the thrones were placed and the judgment was set." Revelation is a book of judgment, and he who forgets this loses the key to interpreting the Apocalypse correctly. The seals, the trumpets, and the bowls are all judgments—the well-known messianic woes, and the birth pangs of a new world.

Again we must remind ourselves that Revelation is an enlarged Olivet Discourse. That sermon was given during Christ's judgment week (see John 12:31). His discourses and acts in those last days were all characterized by judgment. The cleansing of the temple, the cursing of the fig-tree, the woes on the Pharisees, the parables concerning the destruction of the keepers of the vineyard, the marriage of the king's son, plus the inspection of the guests, the unfaithful servant cut in sunder, the sleeping virgins, the stewards giving account, and the sheep and the goats—all were permeated by the same motif of judgment. Therefore, the Olivet sermon is all of a piece with its setting. This enlarged edition, John's Apocalypse, is characterized by the same theme.

Neither are the topics of the Olivet sermon and the Apocalypse novel. They had been well known for a long time. The Old Testament, the Apocrypha, and the Pseudepigrapha all use and re-use the same themes.

How can a book be so full of the crucified Christ, so permeated with references to the Lamb and yet be shrill with judgment? The ideas are not really disparate. Privilege determines responsibility, and to whom much is given, much is expected. And God has given much—in his Son. See John 3:18,19 and 3:36.

It is fashionable to avoid talking of the wrath of God. Karl Barth for years neglected the theme and likewise most contemporary theologians. But the Apocalypse knows no such finicky reserve. There are sixteen references to wrath here. Moderns have forgotten that the most loved verse of the Bible warns that unbelievers will "perish." The sun that melts wax also hardens clay. No one can be the same after hearing the gospel. They are either better or worse—much better or much worse. But God's wrath is not irritable and moody like ours. It is the inevitable recoil of holiness against all that would destroy.

What we will read in coming chapters is a summary, dark with woe, about eschatological events. Revelation is not intended to sketch a successive outline of many centuries of light and shadow. It is almost all shadow because it chiefly pertains to the very last days. This view is neither futurism nor dispensationalism—it is fidelity to the evidence of the book itself. These last events have cast their shadows before and so the book has significance for all ages. It has most significance when we see it as a portrayal of the very last things—events that will accompany the universal proclamation of the gospel.

Granted that the following chapters are large with judgment, how shall we interpret the first set of woes—the seven seals? Let us first remember those to whom the vision was originally addressed. Christians of the first century were a troubled community without worldly wealth, influence, or might. And they seemed poised on the edge of an onslaught that could only result in widespread, if not universal martyrdom. All things seemed to warn of a coming worldwide Calvary. How does this vision of the seals have relevance for them?

Does John give us some clues by the literary relationship he expresses between this sixth chapter and other parts of his book? We observe parallels between it and chapters one and nineteen. In chapter one we found the dominant impression conveyed by the initial vision was one of light—sun, fire, lamps, stars—all were mentioned. Three times, white was used to describe the gleaming figure of the Priest-King, the Son of Man of Daniel's vision, though now sharing characteristics of the Ancient of Days. Therefore, at the portals of the Apocalypse, the theme was presented of light displacing darkness as the Lord worked through his church. Now in chapter six we have the conquering warrior on the white horse. The usual term for white in Revelation has the significance of "shining" and is applied to things glorious. In Revelation it is always used in relationship to heavenly affairs. So the vision in chapter one, and that of six, as well as 10, 12, and 18 all begin with emblems of light symbolizing the church's warfare against the darkness of this world. The white horse is in perfect harmony with the Son of Man whose hair is gleaming and glorious, the heavenly messenger of ten whose face was as the sun, the woman clothed with the sun and stars and the moon under her feet, and the angel of chapter 18 who causes the whole earth to be brightened with his splendour.

Another clue is the fact that the woes of the seals (and the trumpets and bowls) are covenant woes. Leviticus 26 is a vital chapter for interpreting this book. Repeatedly in it we read of punishment "seven times more" for those who do not respond to God's mercies. Revelation 4:3 refers to the covenant rainbow—a reference to the covenant made not just with Israel at Sinai, but the whole world at the Fall. Some have seen an allusion to the covenant symbol in the bow in the hands of the first rider—the significance of the covenant bow in Genesis 9 is that the arrow of wrath has been discharged away from earth.

The rainbow seen in Revelation 4:3, with its mingling of sunshine and shower, portrays God's nature of love and justice, mercy and holiness, and consequently the essence of all that happens on earth. Christ is both Lamb and Lion; the *Goel* (kinsman-redeemer) is both Redeemer and Avenger. While the white horse offers life eternal, the pale steed brings death and the grave. Truth in history, as everywhere else, must speak both in terms of light and shadow.

The sealed book has been variously interpreted—the book of life, the book of Revelation itself, the book of destiny, a testament or will, the title deed of the world, etc. Scripture itself, here as ever, is the best guide. See Jeremiah 32:6-14; Leviticus 25:13; Psalm 74:2; Luke 24:21; Ruth 4; Ephesians 1:13; Job 19:25-29; 27:13; and Daniel 12:13. These passages speak of redemption as illustrated by Old Testament procedures.

We think Seiss is right when he comments on this issue:

> It is not ecclesiastical history, which this book is introduced to foreshow, but something to which all ecclesiastical history is only the prelude and introduction, and which Scripture calls "The redemption of the purchased possession."
>
> The word redemption comes to us, and takes its significance from certain laws and customs of the ancient Jews. Under these laws and customs it was impossible to alienate estates beyond a given time … the next of kin … could step in and redeem it.

Apocalypse, pp. 403-404

Seiss comments on the way sin has alienated our inheritance in this world but that Christ our Redeemer has now taken possession for us. The sealed book in John's vision symbolizes the title deeds of the lost world. The removing of the seals represents the steps whereby the Saviour returns to us our lost inheritance.

We must not lose sight of the central image—the slain but now powerful Lamb who becomes a lion. Christ is our warrior-king. In the seals we see Christ mainly as the Redeemer, caring for his own amid the outpouring of judgments. In the Trumpets (where we find no reference to the Lamb) Christ shall be seen as the Redeemer's alter ego—the Avenger.

Last, consider the parallel between Revelation 6 and Revelation 19. The sequence in the first is 1. a white horse; 2. a great sword; 3. balances of judgment, and 4. death and the grave. In the second we read of him on a white horse with a sword, and he comes to judge. His vesture is that of death. In 6:10 the question arose, "How long, O Lord, holy and true, do you not judge and avenge our blood?" But in 19:2 we read, "He has judged and avenged the blood of his servants."

Fearful yet faithful servants of Christ can find much to encourage and inspire in this vision of the sealed book. After all, the Sovereign of the universe is on our side, and he counts the hairs of our heads.

Chapter Three
The Sounding of Trumpets

○ ○

And I saw the seven angels who stand before God, and to
them were given seven trumpets.

Revelation 8:2

Read Revelation chapters 8-9.

The seven churches and the seven seals are now succeeded by the seven
trumpets. To the seven churches, Christ manifests himself as Priest, Prophet,
and King; in the seven seals we see him as Prophet, King, and Priest; but in
the Trumpets he is King, Priest, and Prophet. As Priest he tended the lamps,
as Prophet he foretold the destiny of the church and the world, and as King
he rules and judges.

In general most of the interpretations that have been offered for the
trumpets are disappointing. Uncertainty, vagueness, and comparative
irrelevance confront the reader. Some exegetes are honest enough to confess
that they have no idea what the trumpets are about. The various expositions
certainly do not agree, and the range of divergence is amazing.

The very worst interpretations come from Historicists—those who
customarily indulge in selecting historical dates (despite Acts 1: 7) and
lunging at the Papacy. All of these may be quickly despatched. Typically
Revelation 9:15 is interpreted as pointing to a time period of over 390 years,
but the Greek clearly indicates a point of time, not a period. See all modern
translations.

This means that the laboured exegesis of Barnes, Newton, Litch, Uriah
Smith and others will not do. Some, such as Litch, have even forgotten the

calendar change during the period they fixed upon, despite the fact that the dropping of 10 days was involved.

Then there is the use of the number "ten thousand times ten thousand." That figure can never be applied to armies of the past or the present. It is a figure that fits demonic legions, but not human ones. The king over this vast horde is said to be the angel of the bottomless pit, and his name is the Destroyer. This is one of Satan's titles in Scripture, and in this setting applies better to him than to all others.

Few scholars doubt that chapters 10-19 sketch the last crisis of history, and it is obvious that Revelation 8 and 9 use similar symbolism in many respects to Revelation 16, but with this difference—the plagues depicted here are sometimes limited to one-third of the world. Also these tragedies are intended to lead men to repentance and salvation. On the contrary, the plagues of Revelation 16 are the last and offer no opportunity for changing sides. Therefore the trumpets point to preliminary judgments during probationary time, while the plagues will follow the close of mercy's intervention.

Such judgments as overtook Jerusalem and Rome, the apostate Christian world, have occurred in miniature throughout the ages. The very progressiveness of the series implies that the course so traced may be as appropriate for individuals as for groups, in all places and in all ages. As surely as the seven letters and the seals have recurring significance, so also do the trumpets. In one sense they run parallel with the seals from John's day to the close of mankind's day. They terminate with the proclamation that the kingdoms of this world have become the kingdoms of Christ.

The allusions to the fallen stars which link with the account of Satan's apostasy in chapter 12 indicate that the trumpets will have much to say about the punitive effects of apostasy. The chief exegetical keys, however, are found in the relationship between the trumpet-imagery and the Creation, the plagues on Egypt, the fall of Jericho, the ushering in of the Jubilee, the contrast between the horses of chapter six and those of nine, and the parallelism to the seven last plagues found in Revelation 16.

Genesis chapter one sets forth much that is embodied as imagery in Revelation eight and nine. Therefore we are now being confronted with the undoing of Creation—the destruction of vegetation, judgments upon the earth and sea, darkening of the sun, moon, and stars, and death to the inhabitants of sea and land. The Trumpets picture the days of Creation in reverse, a reduction to the original chaos as the birth pangs of a new world.

The plagues of Egypt find an obvious parallel with at least five of the Trumpets, and we must not forget the blowing of the seven rams' horns as trumpets for seven days before Jericho's fall, paving the way for the Israelites to inherit Canaan. The Holy Spirit intimates here that the Jericho of this world must also fall by the judgments of God before the saints enter upon immortality and their eternal inheritance.

What shall we say specifically of the fifth and sixth of these judgments? Some of the symbolism is easily unlocked by other passages of Scripture. See Zechariah chapter one, for example, with its use of horses. Because of the strength and swiftness of ancient steeds, Bible seers were led to employ them as a symbol for supernatural powers in action (see Psalm 68:16).

None would claim, however, that Revelation nine pictures the work of the angels of God. Rather they are the opposite numbers of those in Revelation six. Revelation has many instances of contrast such as the Lamb versus the beast, the true Trinity versus the false (dragon, beast, and false prophet), Jesus versus Apollyon, the woman clothed with the sun versus the woman clothed in purple and scarlet, God's seal or mark versus the mark of the beast, the marriage supper of the Lamb versus the supper of the birds of prey, and Jerusalem versus Babylon, etc.

The seven seals presented the future particularly from the viewpoint of the true people of God. They are, so to speak, in the eye of the storm. The seals echo Christ's forecast of the victorious spread of the gospel to all nations, and culminate in the company gathered out and sealed for salvation. But also they warned of opposition to that gospel, and the subsequent loss of peace in a troubled world whose violence is an attempt to quieten its conscience. The third seal had pictured spiritual famine, but also God's care over his own. The balances not only told of scarcity, but also of increasing strictness in judgment, and thus the fourth horse carried the rider of death and scattered everywhere the disease of spiritual pestilence that leads to Hades. Then the following two seals encompassed the cry of persecuted saints and heaven's reply in the convulsed heavens, blackened sun, and falling stars—omens of the Last Judgment as Christ appears. The interlude of chapter seven, seen in its relationship to the last verses of six, follows the same pattern as Matthew 24:29-31.

Now the trumpets follow the same ground from another viewpoint. Trumpets speak of war and judgment, whereas seals speak of religious mystery and legal proceedings. We find no Lamb mentioned amidst the trumpet scenes, for these judgments are aimed at those who have not responded to the Lamb's sacrifice.

The final fling of Antichrist is brought to view in the fifth and sixth plagues and likewise in the climactic woes of the trumpets. It is significant that both mention the Euphrates—that symbol of evil and potential invasion.

In this regard, it is important to remember that Revelation 11 is also part of the sixth trumpet, and it pictures the final attack on the church by Antichrist, as well as the torment, earthquake, and deaths sent to awaken the deceived multitudes. Similarly, the famous eschatological passage of 2 Thessalonians 2 speaks of a final world rebellion and its results. Both the climactic bowls and the prophecy of Paul accord with our Lord's prediction of spiritistic signs and wonders immediately preceding his return, leading men to their last rebellion against heaven. The sixth trumpet points to this.

Revelation nine presents a satanic work that will counterfeit the final work of the Holy Spirit (18:1-4). The supernatural powers of Revelation nine come from the bottomless pit, from the abyss, and from the abode of death. This is the opposite source to that from which the horses of Revelation six proceeded. Furthermore, the powers of Revelation nine have a king over them called Abaddon or Apollyon (meaning the Destroyer). The details of the locusts and horses serve only to stress certain truths regarding these demons. They are, for example, a great army as multitudinous as locusts, as malicious as scorpions, dominant as kings, intelligent as men, wily as women, fierce as lions, and resistless as soldiers in armor.

The Trumpets are distinct from the Seals in that they are directed particularly against those rejecting the gospel, whereas with the seals both parties suffered. Here God by his judgments besieges the Jericho of this world to bring it down either by penitence or destruction, in order that his people might possess the earth.

The Trumpets refer to the rivers and fountains of water, and the sun, moon, and stars—further emblems of the gospel and its blessings. See John 4:14; 7:37-39; and Ezekiel 47. When men do not appreciate the gospel, bitterness and darkness result. Furthermore, to reject the gospel and the seal of the enlightening Spirit is to be left without defense in the onslaught of error from the pit and its demons. It is safer to play with forked lightning than to reject the truth and mercy of God.

Trumpet one is a clear allusion to catastrophic war on a large scale. The fire of wrath and war kindled by the holiness of God consumes and desolates. This plague has fallen again and again in history calling men to awake to eternal realities as creatures on the verge of death and judgment. Trumpet two uses "as" or "like," telling us clearly that it is a symbolic portrayal. A mountain is a familiar symbol of a kingdom, and is used of Babylon the oppressor and is suitable for the Roman Empire. The sea is a frequent symbol of the nations of earth. Next the agencies of blessing to man become a means of cursing. The heavenly warrior in his besiegement of the world curtails its blessings that some might see the connection between their sins and their suffering.

The plagues of God first affect man's physical life, but after the first two trumpets we have a sequence of deepening calamities involving mind and spirit, until the day of penitence is past. Those who reject the seal of truth become subject to error and the prey of the denizens of hell.

The warnings of God, such as those found in these chapters, are messages of love, pleading with men and women to turn back from their advance towards death and eternal loss. The Eternal loves the wicked and having died for them now pleads that his sacrifice might not be in vain.

Chapter Four

Take It and Eat It

∘ ∘

So I went to the angel and asked him to give me the little scroll. He said to me, "Take it and eat it. It will turn your stomach sour, but in your mouth it will be as sweet as honey."

Read Revelation chapters 10-12.

"All sad sights are relieved in the Apocalypse by the vision of Christ and peace" (Isaac Williams). As one comes to the end of the ninth chapter with its account of eschatological trauma for the whole world, certain questions inevitably arise. What has been happening to the church? Has it been faithful to its task? The tenth chapter answers such questions.

Central to this glorious vision in the opening verses is the little open book. It symbolizes the fulfilment of Mark 13:10 and Matthew 24:14. This passage is parallel to Revelation 14:6 and 18:1-4.

> And the gospel must first be preached to all nations.
> Mark 13:10

> And this gospel of the kingdom will be preached to the whole world as a testimony to all nations, and then the end will come.
> Matthew 24:14

> Then I saw another angel flying in midair, and he had the eternal gospel to proclaim to those who live on the earth—to every nation, tribe, language and people.
> Revelation 14:6

After this, I saw another angel coming down from heaven. He had great authority, and the earth was illuminated by his splendor. With a mighty voice he shouted.

> "Fallen! Fallen is Babylon the Great! she has become
>   a home for demons
> And a haunt for every evil spirit, a haunt for every
>   unclean and detestable bird,
> For all the nations have drunk the maddening wine
>   of her adulteries.
> The kings of the earth committed adultery with
>   her, and the merchants of the earth grew rich
>   from her excessive luxuries."

Then I heard another voice from heaven say:

> "Come out of her my people, so that you will not
>   share in her sins, so that you will not receive
>   any of her plagues...."
> Revelation 18:1-4

We would emphasize that this passage (Revelation 10-12), if put with Revelation 6:10 to which it alludes in verse seven, explains the whole philosophy of Christian chronology. The Lord has tarried only because the Word of his grace has not yet echoed through all creation. He cannot return until the conflict, which began with one family in one place, expands to take in every family in every part of the earth. The universal proclamation will produce a harvest ripe for the gathering—a harvest of saints trusting wholly in the merits of Christ and loyal unto death, and a harvest of impenitent sinners who show that they have settled permanently into error by sentencing to death those who have offered them life. See Revelation 14:14-16 and Mark 4:29. In 6:10, the suffering saints are assured that when the world's cup of iniquity is full, then the people and ways of God will be vindicated by the return of Christ. This global display of the fruit of both good and evil is essential for the ending of the great controversy. It will manifest to the principalities and powers of heavenly places the manifold wisdom of God and so ensure that throughout the infinite dominions of the Creator sin will not rise up the second time.

In verses 8-11 John personifies the Church of God—the two witnesses about to be described. Like Ezekiel of old, he consumes the divine message, though ultimately it means bitterness. His is a commission that would include both joy and sorrow, as the following chapter makes clear.

The preaching of the open scroll results in the experience set forth in the eleventh chapter. The bitterness indicates the suffering coming to those who proclaim the sweet tidings of the gospel. And this suffering is to be worldwide for it is promised that there shall be no more delay.

The temple of God, the holy city, the two witnesses, the two olive trees and the lampstands all symbolize the witnessing church. They witness to the truths contained in the Law and the Prophets (alluded to by references to the experiences of Moses and Elijah in verses six to seven) and they, like Joshua and Zerubbabel of old, have priestly and royal prerogatives and duties. But they are slain by the angry world. It would be impossible for people of all nations to behold two literal corpses in the literal streets of literal Jerusalem. The worldwide church is signified.

This chapter gives John's inspired understanding of what the future holds for believers. Soon they are to enter upon the great tribulation (the final worldwide Calvary), similar to that of the days of Antiochus Epiphanes, but now to be global. (In the days of Antiochus, to keep the fourth commandment of the Decalogue brought death.) Those who refuse to "worship the beast and his image" will be slain by the beast from the abyss, just as those who refused to receive the mark of the ivy branch and conform to the false worship surrounding the image of Antiochus were martyred in the second century B.C. The spirit of Jewry, which crucified Christ, is to be the spirit of the entire world in their opposition to the church.

The beast is Antichrist, as the later chapters make clear. He is victorious for 1260 days, and during that time he treads down the worshippers in the sanctuary. See Mark 13:14 and Matthew 24:15. He is from the abyss in the sense that Christ by his victory on Calvary has inflicted upon Satan and his representatives a mortal wound. Later the rising from the abyss indicates a renewal of persecution, a healing of the death wound. Verses seven and eight point to the same crisis as 13:11-18. That passage also alludes to the healing of the mortal wound of the beast, and that healing is made manifest by the beast's renewed persecution. All attempts to apply this healing to experiences of the papacy minimize the significance of the Cross. See Hebrews 2:14.

Verses 9-13 point to the vindication of the martyred witnesses. At the coming of Christ his saints will be raised glorified.

The reference in verse 13 to a great earthquake indicates that the silencing of the witnessing church, marked by the world's rejoicing, is abruptly terminated by terror. The impact of the withdrawal of the Word and the Spirit becomes apparent. Society is shaken and terrified, and many die in the panic. This is the equivalent of the withdrawal of the benevolent "hinderer" in Second Thessalonians chapter two.

Revelation 11 sets forth in seed form all that is to be enlarged in the following chapters, and in so doing it indicates the manner in which these later chapters are to be interpreted.

Forty-two months, or 1260 days, is a symbol recurring in chapters 11-13. Why forty-two? It is for several reasons. First, this was the length of time in the persecution by Antiochus Epiphanes, the most terrible experience of Israel between the Babylonian Captivity and the Advent of Christ. Second, 42 years was the length of the wanderings of Israel in the desert. (After two years they were sentenced to 40 more.) Third, it is the length of the great apostasy in the days of Jezebel, when the heavens were shut for 42 months. Fourth, it is the number of stations of Israel in the wilderness. Thus Matthew shortened Christ's genealogy in order to make it conform to Israel's pilgrimage. Fifth, our Lord's ministry to Israel, despised and rejected of men, was 42 months. In chapters 11 and 12 the experience of the Church is plainly modelled on the experience of its Head. Forty-two months equals three-and-a-half years, a broken seven, symbolic of unrest, trouble, and persecution.

With chapter 12 we approach the central section of the Apocalypse. From 12:1 to 14:14 is the keystone of the book. It also introduces the second half of Revelation. Here the seven mystic figures begin—the sun-clothed woman, the Red Dragon, the Man-child, the beast from the sea, the beast from the land, the Lamb on Mount Zion, and the Son of God on the cloud. The central verses of the book in 12:10-12 are those of doxology—truly a gospel song.

Satan's henchmen are presented in chapter 13 (the Antichrist chapter), the beast from the sea, and the beast from the land. This is the antitype of Christ's antagonists—the devil, Rome, and Judaism. The first beast represents the nations of the world united against God's people. The second beast symbolizes the apostate religion of the world. As church and State led of Satan united against Christ, so it is to be again. As the Triumphal Entry polarized Israel, so the final proclamation of the gospel will polarize the world.

The second beast will be professedly Christian for it has two horns like a lamb, though when it speaks it does so as a dragon. It will claim to do the work of an Elijah, even bringing fire down from heaven as he did. Thus it comes in the guise of a reform to save the world, a reform claiming miraculous Pentecostal fire. Its work is parallel to that of the Two Witnesses, as their counterfeit. Just as the dragon counterfeits God, and the first beast counterfeits Christ, so this lamblike antagonist counterfeits the Holy Spirit. To apply this symbol to any specific nation today is to miss the depth of its meaning.

What is the Mark of the Beast? These last verses of the chapter characterize the last days when the issue of worship shall divide the world, a time when

Christians will be forbidden to enact the outward signs and symbols of the gospel they cherish. Instead, coercion will be used to urge them into idolatrous worship and its forms. The contrasting seal of God will be placed on all those who worship God as the Creator of heaven and earth, and who in allegiance keep his commandments (see 14:7,12 and 12:17).

In the Old Testament the fourth commandment was the shield against all idolatrous systems. It is the largest, the most elaborate, and the first positive law of the Ten. To get rid of it from one end one would have to climb over three other eternal laws, and to get rid of it from the other end one would need to clamber over six such laws. The central Hebrew words of the Decalogue are "the seventh day is the Sabbath." Christ observed it in life and in death. Of the approximately 150 references to the Sabbath in the Bible, only one can be construed as negative (Colossians 2:16), but not by the best New Testament scholars. To wipe out the Sabbath on the basis of Colossians 2:16, one would also have to wipe out all eating and drinking (see the context). The most influential and most saintly of all Christians in all ages have ever advocated the importance and permanence of the fourth commandment.

Never was there as an age that needed the Sabbath so desperately. In our time even Christian churches give it scant respect. A single hour's attendance is made to represent the keeping holy of God's day. But see Isaiah 58:13,14.

The first conflict on earth was over worship, and so the last shall be. Associated with the first was a mark and again this is to be the case. The mark was a sign of protection (see also Exodus 12 and Ezekiel 9). The mark of the beast and the seal of God are opposites. The former is the counterfeit of the latter. Both have an inward reality and an outward form. The inward reality of the seal of God is the reflection of the divine character made possible by the sealing work of the Holy Spirit. The outward sign is set forth in the fourth commandment where alone are we told who made the world and the extent of his rights over it. This is the only commandment that speaks of holiness— the sign of God's own character. The inward reality of the mark of the beast is the reflection of the murderous character of Satan, the first Antichrist.

The seal of God is shown to be a protecting sign. See Revelation 7. And the mark of the beast offers protection to those engaged in false worship.

In other ages the test was over worship but the outward signs were the mark of the beast to Christians. However, during the Middle Ages for many Protestants the test was over the Mass. Thus Revelation 20 comprehends all who have refused to bow to false worship, whatever the issue in time.

It is of more than passing interest that the last century's most well known theologian wrote encomiums on the fourth commandment perhaps unequalled by any other writer before or since. We quote him:

This is the most detailed of all the Ten Commandments. With the second, it outwardly characterised most clearly the attitude of Old Testament man, his obedience or disobedience. Understood and grasped in its new—or rather its true form, in its first and final meaning, it was surprisingly quickly and self-evidently seen to be valid and authoritative in New Testament Christianity as a rule which must naturally apply forthwith to the old, the new, the one people of God

...

In general, theological ethics have handled this command of God, or the one command of God in this particular application, with a casualness and feebleness, which certainly do not match its importance in Holy Scripture or its decisive material significance .... It is thus to be placed at their head.

...

It demands that man know himself only in his faith in God, that he will work and express himself only in this imposed and not selected renunciation, and that on the basis of this renunciation he actually dares in it all to be a new creature, a new man. This is the astounding requirement of the Sabbath commandment.

De Quervain is only too right in this respect. "Where the holy day becomes the day of man, society and humanity wither away and the demons rule."

These quotations come from *Church Dogmatics,* volume III. We recommend that the reader, if he can, read the whole of the section on the fourth commandment. We suggest also that the story of the Edenic temptation found in *Perelandra* (later known as *Voyage to Venus*) by C.S. Lewis be closely studied.

The inspired opening chapter of the Bible has overwhelming importance for our materialistic age. All other doctrinal truths have their spring in the fact of creation. This does not mean that we must assent to such beliefs as a 6,000-year-old world, but it does mean that faith in the supernatural as authenticated by the fact of creation is a pillar for spiritual sanity. Science in the last 50 years, by its discovery of the anthropic principle and the miraculous

DNA programs (100,000,000 times more compact than any device invented by man, with every cell containing enough information to fill 100,000,000 pages of *Encyclopaedia Britannica*), has removed all legitimate bases for doubt. See the book *In the Beginning* by Henri Blocher for the most up-to-date understanding of the significance of Genesis chapter one.

The essence of the final crisis is no mere ritualistic observance, but absolute loyalty to the Christ of Calvary. Eden's test seemed to be over an insignificant trifle, yet on the hinge of that trifle swung the door of destiny. The last test, as with the first, may also be over what at first seems trivial— but obedience to the exact requirements of the eternal God is the primary duty of all rational creatures. Only those constrained as Paul (2 Corinthians 5:14) and for the same reason are enabled to preserve the delicate balance of responsibility towards both God and man, avoiding the terrible brood of both pharisaism and antinomianism.

666—the Number of the Beast. Cataracts of nonsense have been written on this topic. In the Old Testament the number six is frequently associated with what is evil when man is under the dominion of Satan. Both man and the serpent were created on the sixth day. Its triple form here no doubt signifies the intensity of satanic domination. When secularism and materialism rule the world, its demise is near.

Chapter Five

The Hour of His Judgment Is Come

○ ○

He said in a loud voice, "Fear God and give him glory, because the hour of his judgment has come. Worship him who made the heavens, the earth, the sea and the springs of water."

Revelation 14:7

Read Revelation chapters 14-16.

It is in this section that we read of Armageddon, the climactic battle between good and evil ended by the coming of Christ and his angels. The word does not occur earlier but the theme runs through the whole book. We miss much if we miss the warning of Revelation that the scenes of the Sanhedrin, Pilate's judgment hall, Calvary, and the empty tomb are soon to find their consummation on a worldwide scale. As Austin Farrer wrote years ago, "The substance of the last things and the substance of the Passion are the same." All references to Antichrist, including such titles as "The Abomination of Desolation," "the man of sin," and "the little horn," point to the denouement. Not only the prophecies of Daniel and Revelation, but the Olivet Discourse and 2 Thessalonians, have much to say about this last conflict.

We now live on the eve of Armageddon. No weapon that has ever been invented has failed of employment. Nuclear warfare may lie ahead for the world, plus the multiplying of national and natural disasters because of climate damage and the dangerous misuse of modern technology, enabling a very few men now to kill millions. Religion may be sought as the cure for these threats, but it will be the religion of human idolatry that bypasses the Creator of heaven and earth.

Revelation 14:6-12 must be read with the thirteenth chapter. Here is the most fearful warning of Scripture to save men from the destiny waiting all who refuse the worship of the Creator and receive the mark of the beast. Observe that "the everlasting gospel" has primacy in this warning, for only the conviction of the infinite love of God for weak fallible sinners can nerve us to resist evil even at the price of life itself. The Babylon in this passage is the symbol for all false religion, especially good religion turned sour.

From the time Revelation was written Christians have believed they were delivering to the world the warning message of 14:6-12. It had significance for those ordered to participate in false worship by offering incense to Caesar. Later, in the Middle Ages, the crisis was over participation in the Mass, but just ahead of us lies the consummation when this message has its fullest application, as men must choose between the worship of Antichrist or of Christ the Creator and Redeemer.

For commentary on the essence of the threefold message read John 3:36 and 16:8-11. To believe on the Son is to be delivered from sin, and guilt, and wrath. It is to have eternal life now, and a perfect imputed righteousness. It is to possess in the present the favourable verdict of the Last Judgment. This is the first angel's message. But to fail to believe, to abide in Babylon, and to live by its false gospel of creature-centered worship, is to fail of true life. This is the second angel's message. Ultimately that attitude means that the wrath of God, his inevitable recoil against all destroying evils, a wrath that already rests upon the unbeliever, becomes a consuming fire. This is the third angel's message. And remember that God warns in order that his warning may not find fulfilment—if men repent and turn from evil.

In the literary structure of Revelation, which must not necessarily be given chronological significance, the seventh seal unfolded in seven trumpets, and the seventh trumpet unfolds in the seven last plagues. Chronologically, the parallel passages of 6:12-17; 8:1-5; 11:19 and 16:18 show that the seals and the trumpets and the plagues end at the same place, but only the first two series, which border on probationary time, begin at the identical moment. With the plagues mercy has ceased to plead, and they fall upon those who have planned the attack on the church pictured in 13:11-18. This attack is the raging of the nations, which belongs to the second woe, while the plagues are the third woe or seventh trumpet.

Commentators as a whole are less satisfying on the seven last plagues than on any other section of the book except Revelation chapters 8, 9, and 20. Most historicists have located the commencement of the plagues either in the days of Luther or the French Revolution. Their itemized suggestions, when read in the first quarter of the twenty-first century, seem like a comic strip. Other historicists who apply them to the last judgments on the impenitent have sometimes mingled their exegesis with fanciful interweaving of expository hangovers from the days of Bishop Newton and the more recent journalistic "yellow peril" ravings. Therefore one finds extreme literalizing of Euphrates, Megiddo, the kings of the east, and the like.

On the other hand, preterists have applied the bowls to a series of judgments with a primary termination in the decade that witnessed the death of Nero and the fall of Jerusalem, with an ultimate application to the destruction of paganism in the days of Constantine.

Dispensational futurists literalize the plagues as much as possible. There will be oceans of blood, an increase of sun temperature followed by its darkening, and ultimately the coming of the oriental hordes descending upon the Middle East for the last great battle, with the plain of Esdraelon as the central point of the conflict.

Let us keep in mind the sequence of the chapters in this second half of Revelation. The last verse of the first half (11:18) had spoken about the raging of the nations and God's subsequent wrath. These are the chief subjects of the second half of the book. Revelation 12 and 13 sketch the raging of the nations as they attack the Man-child, the woman who brought him forth, and the remnant of the woman's seed. The serpent directs all of this. The rage that was introduced in chapter 12 is enlarged in the following chapter. Next we would expect the wrath of God, and we find that in chapters 14-20. In general terms the judgment of God is announced and summarized in chapter 14, then delineated under the symbolism of seven last plagues in chapters 15 and 16, and still further delineated in chapters 17 to 20, as the harlot (Babylon), the beast, and the false prophet in chapter 19, and the dragon in chapter 20 come to their end. While the first half of Revelation was general in its prophetic outlines, this second half is increasingly detailed. But it is in chapter 16 that we have the first comprehensive picture of the execution of judgment upon the lost.

But chapter 16 has a much more important significance than merely a detailed portrayal of judgment. It enshrines "a supreme moment in the history of the Church and the end of the world." The final gathering on the battlefield of Armageddon is the peak to which everything else rises. This is the last great conflict between good and evil, the same as that in Revelation 13:11-18. In Revelation 16:13-15 there is a definite regression to events prior to the falling of the plagues. Underlining the significance of this whole section is the shrill warning, "Lo, I am coming like a thief. Blessed is he who is awake, keeping his garments that he may not go naked and be seen exposed." This is a trumpet call to professed believers to be ready for the imminent eschatological crisis, which will place them with one army or the other and determine their destiny forever. The verse is an allusion to Matthew 24:42-44.

No interpretation of Revelation 16 will be satisfactory that does not recognize its allusions to the following Old Testament types:

1. The plagues on Egypt prior to the deliverance of the Exodus. (Revelation 16 points to a final Exodus prior to the inheritance of the eternal Canaan.)

2. The protecting cloud of darkness over Israel when about to be destroyed by the Egyptians (Exodus 14:19,20).

3. The Megiddo battles of Israel's history (Judges 4, see 5:19; 1 Kings 18:40; 2 Kings 23:29 and Zechariah 12:11).

4. The second Exodus, after the fall of Babylon under the attack of Cyrus. (The language of 16:12 is certainly borrowed from Isaiah, particularly 11:15 and 44:27,28. See also Jeremiah 50:28 and 51:36).

5. Joshua's coming from the east to enter Canaan, and the invasion of Babylon by Cyrus, God's Messiah from the east (Isaiah 45:1-4 and 41:2). Compare Matthew 24:27 and Ezekiel 43:2.

6. The conflict of Ahab and Jezebel with Elijah on Carmel (the false prophets were slain at Megiddo.) 1 Kings 18:40.

7. God's destruction of Israel's attackers by hailstones (Exodus 9:18 and Joshua 10:11).

8. The destruction of Babylon as sketched in Daniel, Isaiah, and Jeremiah. (It must not be forgotten that all the plagues are said to be Babylon's. See Revelation 18:4.)

9. The gathering of the kings to battle by evil spirits. Compare Revelation 16:13 with 13:13-15 and 2 Chronicles 18:19-21.

10. The Day of Atonement ritual (Leviticus 16).

Many of the features of the Calvary Atonement are in this frightening chapter, because all that was fulfilled by Calvary is now to be consummated. The blood, the darkness, and the fierce heat of the sun—emblematic of the wrath of God—and demons incite men to their last conflict with God. Why are they here? Their presence is to warn men that if they reject Christ's Atonement they too will endure the Cross. After probation's close, when terrible wars with their blood-shedding erupt, and nature testifies to man's rebellion by drought and famine, when evil angels control the thoughts of men, then will Calvary be reenacted, but this time on the rejecters of God's love. All must sacrifice. Either we sacrifice our all for Christ our Saviour, or we sacrifice true joy, contentment, and the life to come.

These terrible events, showing the inevitable fruitage of evil, vindicate God's character of truth and goodness. Then will the whole universe sing its anthem of praise to God as predicted in 15:3,4 and 16:5-7. From the minutest atom to the greatest galaxy, the universe will ring with the refrain that God is love.

Chapter Six
The Lamb Will Overcome Them

○ ○

"They will make war against the Lamb, but the Lamb will overcome them because he is Lord of lords and King of kings—and with him will be his called, chosen and faithful followers."

Revelation 17:14

Read Revelation chapters 17-19.

Chapters 17 to 19 repeat the warnings of 15 and 16. Here is a detailed depiction of the destruction of the Antichrist confederacy—the harlot, the beast, the false prophet, and the dragon. Nemesis has come and the judgment is thorough. Babylon is very prominent now, hitherto only twice named (Revelation 14:8 and 16:19). But just who or what is Babylon?

From chapters 11 to 20 Antichrist fills the scene. This is the most prominent feature of the book next to Christ and his Atonement. Antichrist is a genus rather than just an individual. Just as Christ is presented before us 28 times as the Lamb, but also under other titles, so Antichrist appears as the great red dragon, the serpent, the beast, the second beast with two horns, and finally as Babylon. As Revelation is the story of Christ and Antichrist, so it is the tale of two cities—Jerusalem and Babylon—and of two women, one the pure bride clothed in glory, and the other the harlot robed in scarlet. These contrasts must be kept in mind as we consider Revelation chapters 17 and 18, which, along with 16, tell of the fate of Babylon.

The most popular interpretation of Babylon has always been the city of Rome. Does not Revelation speak of "the great city which rules over the kings of the earth," a city which sits on seven hills? These indications, plus the persecution threat from an empire dominated by Rome, are the principal grounds for such an interpretation. We wish to question it. While not denying that Rome was in the prophetic consciousness of the seer of Patmos, we believe that by Babylon he meant apostate religion. Old Jerusalem, not pagan Rome, is the model for his symbolism. This, of course, is no new position to take. Milligan, Carrington, Alford, the *Anchor Bible*, plus a host of others have thus exegeted.

We will summarize the case:

1. To interpret Babylon as the city of Rome is a gross literalism not consistent with the text. It is based chiefly on 17:9. But even the interpreters who favor the Rome view grant that Babylon as a name is not to be taken literally. Furthermore, they assent that the woman is not a literal figure, nor the beast a literal beast. Neither are the heads literal mountains. Yet they have a literal city balanced on top of itself (the seven hills of Rome) though the balancing must be precarious indeed, for five of the hills have fallen, only one is, and the seventh has not yet come. And when it comes, it will last only a short time. See verses 9 and 10. Quite some geographical, and we would add expository, feat!

2. This woman is said to be destroyed by the ten horns of the beast. Thus the beast is, according to the view being examined, the destroyer of its own heart—the city of Rome is destroyed by the Roman Empire! Again, to swallow that is another type of feat.

3. No one would have thought of "that great city" as Rome, had Revelation ended at the close of chapter 14. In 11:8 it is clearly stated that the great city is the one where Christ was crucified, and in the fourteenth chapter it is outside Jerusalem, "the city," where the vintage is trodden. There has been only one city in the book thus far, and it is not Rome. Neither is there a hint in the later chapters that the great city mentioned is a different one.

4. The principle of contrasts should help us. As Antichrist contrasts with Christ, so does Babylon with Jerusalem, and the harlot with the bride. So to understand one clearly is to know the other also. We do know that the pure woman represents the true people of God, the company professing the faith of Jesus, cherishing the commandments of God, and worshipping the Creator of heaven and earth. Therefore the harlot must be an apostate professor of Christ who has trodden underfoot the true gospel, and exchanged it for the wares of the world as it embraces new spouses—the kingdoms of this world. In Revelation 14:1 Zion with her

flock is brought to view, but in verse eight Babylon is warned against. In Revelation chapter 18 the false city of Babylonian religion falls, but in the next chapter the true bride and the true city come to view. As surely as the death of one is the enthronement and supremacy of the other, the first must represent the counterfeit, and the second the true.

5. The book of Revelation's literary and conceptual structure is a copy of Ezekiel's, and in Ezekiel the early chapters lead up to the doom of the harlot, the destruction of apostate Jerusalem, and then at the end, the New Jerusalem comes into view. So in Revelation, the chapters lead up to the burning of Babylon the whore, and then the New Jerusalem emerges.

6. The central event of Ezekiel and of Revelation is the same—the destruction of the harlot. Similarly, in the century of John, the central event has been the fall of Jerusalem.

7. In Revelation, two events are closely linked—the crucifixion of Christ and the subsequent fall of Jerusalem. See 11:8,13 and 19. The order is the same in Revelation 16-18. We read a replay of Christ's last words, "It is done," in 16:17, and then comes the fall of Babylon. See verses 18 and 19. Again the earthquake and hail of chapter 11 are present.

8. The seven last plagues are distinctly affirmed to be Babylon's plagues. See 18:4. But they are all judgments for false apostate religion. Those who had received the mark of the beast now receive the mark of the sore. Those who have refused the pure water of God's fountain of truth now "drink" blood. Those who have rejected the Light of the World walk in darkness after being scorched by the sun. The symbols used are ones that would make sense to Palestinians. The "land" or "earth" to Israel meant their country in contrast to others across the waters. Euphrates was their ideal boundary, and Megiddo their great battlefield. It is apostate Palestine that in symbol receives the plagues, and Palestine is now called Babylon. In the unclean spirits going abroad can be seen the fulfilment of the prophecy of Christ that before the fall of Jerusalem, there would be false prophets and false Christs. Even the special warning in verse 16 is a warning particularly to the temple watchmen, who, if caught asleep, had their clothes set alight.

9. The woman Babylon, even in her dress, counterfeits the sacred priest. She has on her forehead a summary of what she is, as the high priest had on the golden plate on his forehead, "Holiness to the Lord." The desert and

the scarlet are reminders of the High Priest's special work on the Day of Atonement when the goat for Azazel with its strip of crimson wool was sent to the wilderness. The harlot's voluptuous dress is in striking contrast to the pure white of the priest's simple garment on the great day of *Yom Kippur*. Her gold and precious stones are a perversion of the jewels of the breastplate of the priest. The golden cup reminds the beholder of the golden vines inscribed on the gate that opened to the temple, and the sparkling stones of the temple that gleamed like snow. See the contrasting gems of the New Jerusalem in Revelation chapter 21. This "lady" also has had a "ministry" of blood like the priest, but how different in nature and purpose!

10. Her punishment is not just like that of an ordinary harlot who could be stoned (remember the hailstones of Babylon's seventh plague), but she was to be burned with fire. This was the special punishment for a priest's daughter who played the whore. See Revelation 17:16 and Leviticus 21:9.

11. The reference to eating of her flesh in 17:16 points to the portion of the sin offering eaten by the priests.

12. The expression "the great city" was a well-known one for Jerusalem.

13. In the harlot city is found the blood of prophets and saints, and all who have been slain upon the earth. See Revelation 18:24, and compare Christ's words about Jerusalem in Matthew 23:35. Rome did not major in shedding the blood of prophets, though she did very well with the martyrs.

14. If the harlot is not an allusion to apostate Jerusalem, what has happened to that central prediction of Christ's in the Olivet sermon? We have seen its other features repeatedly in this book—what about this one, the most prominent of them all?

The world's final rebellion will not be so much antichristian as pseudo-Christian. The prophetic picture of the harlot riding the beast indicates that, as in the last days of the Old Testament age it was religious apostasy, which preceded the crucifixion of Christ, so in our time it will be Christian apostasy, which will precede the attempted destruction of the saints. Herod and Pilate became friends over the condemned Christ, and divergent elements of our world will find their catalyst in the decision to wipe out a nonconforming Christian minority who are too narrow-minded, much too otherworldly, and too independent in thought. But as it was the betrayal by Jewry of its Messiah that brought its ultimate ruin by fire at the hands of Rome, and so it is now foretold that the first part of the last day execution of judgment will be the burning of the great whore by the kings who formerly supported her. Crime still does not pay, whether it be civil, political, or religious.

In the last verses of chapter 19 we have Armageddon pictured afresh. Christ comes and deals with the beast and the false prophet and their armies. But the dragon is not discussed until the next chapter.

Chapter Seven

They Lived and Reigned with Christ a Thousand Years

○ ○

I saw thrones on which were seated those who had been given authority to judge. And I saw the souls of those who had been beheaded because of their testimony for Jesus and because of the word of God. They had not worshiped the beast or his image and had not received his mark on their foreheads or their hands. They came to life and reigned with Christ a thousand years.

Revelation 20:4

Read Revelation chapter 20.

Some interpreters wished they did not have to comment on this chapter. To start with, every exegete knows that he must upset many people whatever he says. Second, every exegete knows only too well what Caird says about this passage: "More than any other in the book, it has been the paradise of cranks and fanatics on the one hand, and literalists on the other." Well, how many hands does one have? Who wants to be a crank or a literalist? But the legal maxim that abuse does not cancel use is relevant here. Even a clock that is stopped tells the truth twice a day, and it is possible by the law of probability that one or two things fanatics say could have some rhyme or reason. Even they can add two and two and arrive at four. We will not therefore give up arithmetic.

It is quite impossible to approach this chapter without bias. We know what a certain writer is likely to say on this chapter before he writes it, provided we know something about his theological stance.

One thing is encouraging. In many quarters there has been a change of approach in recent years. What was unquestionably orthodoxy in the nineteenth century is no longer so. Premillennialism, though not entirely respectable, is much more so now than then. But the term is still for many a naughty word, because it is frequently equated with dispensationalism and therefore associated with theories such as the secret rapture and pretribulationism. It is vital to point out that such an equation is not necessarily correct. There are many prominent premillennialists who are not dispensational futurists. We add the last word since not all know that some premillennialists are historicists, and others are futurists of the non-dispensational ilk, or merely interpreters courageously rejecting popular prejudices.

The indispensable counters for our study include the terms amillennialism, postmillennialism, and premillennialism. The first group is sure that there will be no real millennium, but that it is figurative of the whole Christian age. The second group anticipate a thousand years of peace on earth after Christ's return. And the third look for Jesus to come before the actual thousand-year period begins.

Here are some basic ideas to keep in mind as we look at Revelation chapter 20.

First, many have rejected premillennialism because of popular extreme views on the subject. Swallowing Hal Lindsey's eschatological views is for many a much harder task than John's digestive feat in Revelation 10.

Second, the amillennial position is strong where it rejects the weaknesses of popular premillennialism. But, exegetically, it is impossible to sustain amillennialism, as many interpreters have confessed in recent years.

Third, the premillennial position is strong where it rejects the exegetical weaknesses of the alternatives. By premillennialist we mean one who believes in a literal millennium bounded at each end by a resurrection from the dead, and introduced by the Second Coming of Christ. We do not mean the dispensationalist position, or that of those who believe the millennium refers to a thousand years of peace on earth.

Fourth, we have a right to expect that the eschatological book of the New Testament might be more detailed in some areas than the rest of Scripture. Therefore, the usual objection—that the New Testament is not elsewhere capable of the interpretation premillennialists give Revelation 20—is not particularly strong.

We think that the spiritualizing of the chapter has been partly due to an ignorance of the real nature of biblical apocalyptic. But there is more.

Not all have observed that the New Testament distinguishes between the dispensation of the Spirit, and the age to come ushered in by the Second Advent. As a rough rule of thumb it can be laid down that where Jesus is visibly present, rather than where the Holy Spirit is the immediate teacher, many other matters also become visibly present. L. F. Were suggested:

> We have shown that the literal application belonged to the days of literal Israel; to the days when the literal glory of God was manifested, and things were upon a literal, national basis. In this "dispensation of the Holy Spirit," the things of Israel apply spiritually. Later, in the eternal kingdom, where the literal glory of the Lord will be revealed again, things pertaining to Israel will once more be literal.
>
> The principle of the triple application enables us to "rightly divide the word of truth." This triple application of the prophecies cause all things to fall into their respective places, in:

1. The national kingdom of God, in the time of the literal economy centered in Jerusalem, and pertaining to the land of Israel.
2. Christ's spiritual kingdom centered in spiritual Jerusalem, the church, and embracing the world.
3. Christ's eternal kingdom with his seat of government literally centered in the New Jerusalem.

The Certainty of The Third Angel's Message, p. 311

No part of Scripture belongs only to the past, present, or future. All of it is relevant in principle in all times. That is why amillennialists can make a good case. Christ did indeed chain the devil at his First Coming, and his kingdom was then established, and Christians have been reigning ever since. See Matthew 12:28; Revelation 12:10; and Ephesians 2:6. But recognizing these truths in our chapter does not suffice to exegete that chapter adequately. Similarly, to recognize that in the description of the new earth is the consummation of present blessings does not deny that the reader can discern his immediate blessings from the description there, but it does deny that such discernment empties the verses of their full store.

We now list our reasons for literalizing the first resurrection of Revelation 20. To establish this establishes also premillennialism.

1. As Ladd says so well:

    > The phrase "they came to life again" is the translation of a single word, *ezesan*. The crux of the entire exegetical problem is the meaning of this word. It is true that the word can mean entrance into spiritual life (John 5:25), but it is not used of any "spiritual resurrection" of the souls of the righteous at death. The word is, however, used of bodily resurrection in John 11:25; Romans 14:9; Revelation 1:18; 2:8; 13:14; and most commentators admit that this is the meaning in verse 5.

    > "The rest of the dead did not come to life again until the thousand years were ended." If *ezesan* in verse 4 designates spiritual life at conversion, or life after death in the intermediate state, we are faced with the problem of the same word being used in the same context with two entirely different meanings, with no indication whatsoever as to the change of meaning.

    > *Revelation*, pp. 265-266

2. *Anastasis* is here translated "resurrection," and the same word is used 39 times in the New Testament always to mean the resurrection of the body. Other words are used to denote a spiritual rising from the death of sin.

3. No Christian doubts that the second or general resurrection described in verse 12 will be literally realized. It is therefore difficult to suppose that the first will be of a different kind.

4. Resurrection must be of the same nature as the death. For example, in Ezekiel chapter 37 the death and resurrection is national, relating to the Jews; in the parable of the prodigal son, the boy who was dead socially and morally becomes alive again socially and morally. It is explicitly said in Revelation 20 that many who rise in the first resurrection had been beheaded literally and physically. Therefore it must be conceded that they are resurrected physically.

5. Inasmuch as those resurrected are said to be those who prior to that time were blessed and holy, this group had already had their spiritual resurrection prior to this event.

6. "Souls" in Scripture often applies to persons living in the flesh (Acts 7:14;

27:37; 1 Peter 3:20, and as for "souls of them," compare 1 Samuel 25:29; Genesis 46:15,18,22,26; and Romans 2:9,10).

7. Paul elsewhere expresses his hope to "attain unto the resurrection of the dead" (Philippians 3:11). If all good and bad were resurrected at the same time it would be impossible to escape the resurrection. The Greek is literally "the out-resurrection from among the dead."

8. Some, including Tregelles, have translated Daniel 12:2 as follows: "Many from among the sleepers of the dust of the earth shall awake; these shall be unto everlasting life; but those [the rest of the sleepers who do not awake at that time] shall be unto shame."

9. Other phraseology indicates two resurrections—"the resurrection of life," John 5:29; of "everlasting life" Daniel 12:2; "of the just" Luke 14:14; "a better resurrection" Hebrews 11:35; "the dead in Christ" 1 Thessalonians 4:16; them "that are Christ's at his coming" 1 Corinthians 15:23—the context shows at each place that the resurrection mentioned is separate from that of the wicked.

10. 1 Corinthians 15:23 suggests a definite order in the resurrection. The word "order" is *tagma*, a military term which means band or regiment. The apostle sees widely separated bands with each man in his proper regiment or division. The Greek word *eita* "then" does not mean immediately after (Mark 4:17; Galatians 2:1).

11. The use of *zaw* elsewhere in Revelation shows that it means "revived," or "lived again," in reference to the body, which had been dead (Revelation 2:8; 13:14; and 20:5).

12. In the phrases "first resurrection" and "second resurrection," a discrepancy as to time is implied. Any great change from a degraded and wretched condition, temporal or spiritual, may indeed be figuratively called a resurrection, a restoration to life, that is, to happiness; but it would be out of the question to name it a first resurrection. This implies of necessity a comparison with a second, in which the first must be like the second in kind.

13. Similarly the *anastasis* (the resurrection) emphasizes not only relation to a second, but its own transcendent importance. Revelation 20:1-8 is a definite link in a chronological chain of text, and it is therefore descriptive of events to follow the Second Advent described in Revelation 19.

14. The analogy of eastern marriage where the groom comes and takes the bride to his father's house for feasting has relevance for Revelation 20, as well as the previous chapter. The millennium will be in heaven, not on earth.

In no case does the Bible speak of the resurrection of anyone but the righteous when Christ comes.

It is no wonder that the famed commentator, Alford, penned the following regarding this passage of Scripture:

> I cannot consent to distort its words from their plain sense and chronological place in the prophecy. ... Those who lived next to the Apostles and the whole Church for 300 years, understood them in the plain literal sense; and it is a strange sight in these days to see expositors who are among the first in reverence for antiquity, complacently casting aside the most cogent instance of unanimity which primitive antiquity presents. As regards the text itself, no legitimate treatment of it will extort what is known as the spiritual interpretation now in fashion. If, in a passage where two resurrections are mentioned, where certain souls lived at the first, and the rest of the dead lived only at the end of a specific period after that first,—if in such a passage the first resurrection may be understood to mean spiritual rising with Christ, while the second means literal rising from the grave;—then there is an end of all significance in language, and Scripture is wiped out as a definite testimony to any thing. If the first resurrection is spiritual, then so is the second, which I suppose none will be hardy enough to maintain: but if the second is literal, then so is the first, which in common with the whole primitive Church and many of the best modern expositors, I do maintain, and receive as an article of faith and hope.

Chapter Eight

He Will Wipe Away Every Tear

○ ○

"He will wipe every tear from their eyes. There will be no
more death or mourning or crying or pain, for the old order
of things has passed away."

Revelation 21:4

Read Revelation chapters 21-22.

We come now to an introduction to a conclusion—a teaspoon's worth of
commentary upon passages sketching an ocean of infinity. Ours is but a
passing reference in time to the soon-coming eternity. The task is beyond
humanity and, like Job, we are constrained to lay a hand over our mouth.
Only a few reflections will be offered.

The Bible speaks of three worlds: the world that then was, the world that
is, and the world that is to come (see 2 Peter 3:7-13). One cannot but be
reminded of the many similarities between the end of the first world and the
beginning of the second, and the end of the second and the commencement of
the third. In Noah's day the warning of the end was given by a faithful remnant
to the multitudes that had forsaken the God of their fathers. Probation closed
for the antediluvians, and simultaneously the believers were safely sealed in
the ark of divine provision. Next came judgment, a storm of wrath, but the
people of God were safely sheltered in a home above the submerged world.
After resting on a mountaintop, the saved emerged to enter the new earth.

So it is to be again. The remnant of the woman's seed will warn the
Babylonian world by the messages of Revelation 14:6-12. Then probation will
close, sealing all men into their eternal destiny. After the seven last plagues,
the faithful will be lifted above the doomed world, safe in the camp of the
saints, the beloved city. At the close of earth's millennial Sabbath of judgment,

during which the globe has existed as a great cemetery, the redeemed return to earth in the New Jerusalem, issuing from it to reign over the whole new world, as Noah's family came from the ark long ago.

The glorious presentation in Revelation 21 and 22 of the new earth is a magnificent conclusion to Scripture. It is John's inspired painting, and his undying melody—a true story about eternity that never suffers for the retelling. A sceptic once proposed that it must have been a matter of great difficulty to begin the Bible. The obvious answer, of course, is that given millenniums, the human race combined could not have devised a better introduction to Holy Writ than the majestic opening of Genesis 1. "In the beginning God created the heavens and the earth." Similarly the conclusion of Scripture has equal grandeur and appropriateness.

It is as though the reader of the Bible has been travelling on a golden ring, and ultimately at Revelation 21 and 22 returned to where he began—with a new world. Instead of the marriage of Adam and Eve, we have here the marriage of the second Adam to his Church. Instead of a day followed by a night, we read of a day that shall know no night. The garden paradise of Eden is replaced by a garden city unlike all the cities of time. Once more we see the tree of life, and again those who partake reflect the image of God, and walk beside crystal streams. But now all testing and trial is over. As the third chapter of the Bible introduced Satan, temptation, sorrow, tears, the curse, and death, so the third last chapter (Revelation 20) ushers all these out of the universe forever. No shadow or blight rests upon a single atom of the earth made new or its inhabitants. It and they are God's new creation. Love, truth, glory, peace, harmony, joy, health and all the other values for which the Church has lived and died now find their eternal consummation.

As we leave the stormy seas of Revelation 20, and enter the calm harbor of chapters 21 and 22, it is like turning from Tchaikovsky's *1812 Overture* to *Swan Lake*.

Now we see the consummation of Daniel's ancient oracle regarding "the anointing of the most holy" (Daniel 9:24). That allusion to the anointing of the Saviour, who tabernacled among us, has its final application in God's infinite condescension, as he tabernacles among the saved. He who walked with Adam and Eve in Paradise, and pilgrimaged with his redeemed through the wilderness and the Galilean hills, now forevermore is the visible King, Brother, and Friend. God himself is the Temple of the new earth.

Much of the language of these chapters is borrowed from Isaiah's picture of the restoration after the Babylonian captivity. That ancient deliverance by the kings of the East was a symbol of a greater redemption, and the return to Palestine imaged the final return of the saved to their eternal home. Other sources include Ezekiel's closing pictures, and promises found in the early chapters of the Apocalypse itself.

The last word comes from Dr W. G. Scroggie:

> Ever present in this world are right and wrong, truth and error, light and darkness, holiness and sin, righteousness and iniquity, heaven and hell, Christ and Satan; and these are in unceasing conflict with one another. Too often it appears that the forces of evil are triumphant, and the Devil seems to dominate the world. It is when this view is depressing us that we should read again the Revelation, and see that Babylon crashes to destruction; that the Beast and the False Prophet are cast into the lake of fire, and that Satan is thrown in the Abyss. Not wrong, and error, and darkness, and sin, and iniquity, and hell, and Satan triumph at last, but right, and truth, and holiness, and righteousness, and heaven, and Christ.
>
> The head, which on earth was crowned with thorns, will be crowned with many diadems. The kingdoms of this world will, before long, become the Kingdom of our Lord and of his Christ, and he shall reign forever and ever.
>
> The final vision is not of Athens and its intellect, nor of Babylon and its luxury, nor of Rome and its power, nor of Paris and its fashion, nor of New York and its commerce, nor of London and its splendor, but is of the New Jerusalem, which stands for character. Harlots, and beasts, and pseudo-prophets, and demons, locusts, frogs, and serpents are all swept away, and the once-slain Lamb is on the throne of the universe, at last and forever triumphant.
>
> This then is the epilogue of the unfolding drama of redemption history, which began in a Garden, ends in a City, and between the two stands a Cross; a Cross by which the tragedy of the Garden has been transformed into the triumph of the City.

The Unfolding Drama of Redemption, p. 412

[For the minute points of exegesis of Revelation, we refer the reader to the two-volume commentary, *Crisis!*, available through Good News Unlimited in Australia and the United States.]